BREV. INTER. CAMPAGNOLO

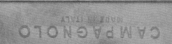

CAMPAGNOLO MADE IN ITALY

CIRCUS

CIRCUS

INSIDE THE WORLD OF PROFESSIONAL BIKE RACING

Camille J McMillan

FOREWORD BY DAVID MILLAR

A Velodrome Book

First published in Great Britain in 2016 by
Velodrome Publishing
A Division of Casemate Publishers
10 Hythe Bridge Street
Oxford OX1 2EW, UK
and
1950 Lawrence Road, Havertown, PA 19083 USA

www.velodromepublishing.com

The Publishers would like to thank:
Paul Hayes-Watkins: design and art direction.
Katy Bravery: copy-editing.

A catalogue record for this book is available from the British Library

Standard Edition ISBN 978-1-911162-03-2
Limited Edition ISBN 978-1-911162-07-0

Printed in China by Printworks Global

To receive regular email updates on forthcoming Velodrome titles,
news and reader offers, please email info@velodromepublishing.com
with 'Velodrome Updates' in the subject field.

For a complete list of Velodrome Publishing titles, please contact:

CASEMATE PUBLISHERS (UK)
Telephone (01865) 241249
Fax (01865) 794449
Email: casemate-uk@casematepublishers.co.uk
www.casematepublishers.co.uk

CASEMATE PUBLISHERS (US)
Telephone (610) 853-9131
Fax (610) 853-9146
Email: casemate@casematepublishing.com
www.casematepublishing.com

For Simone, Hunter and Dorothy

CM

Contents

Opposite
Tour de France, 2013
Col de la Colombière.
1 km to the summit.

Work done for the day
David Millar – 'pro, professional, profi' – chills out
on the team bus on the Tour de France, 2012.

When you're in it you don't see it.

Everything seems normal because extraordinary started being ordinary the moment we turned pro. Because for us, that's all that mattered. It didn't matter what we'd won, where we raced, how good people told us we were, and what greatness we were capable of achieving. We just wanted to be professionals. 'He's a pro'. 'Il est professional'. 'Profi'.

Those of us that made it had a mixed bag – very few of us got what we were told to expect. For that reason, it all became normal. Extraordinary became rare. We just trained, raced, dieted, travelled, slept, occasionally got very drunk... and, if we were fortunate, won a bike race.

Camille saw this – and thankfully for us – captured it.

Tour de France 2011
Individual time trial. Fabian Cancellara, I think.

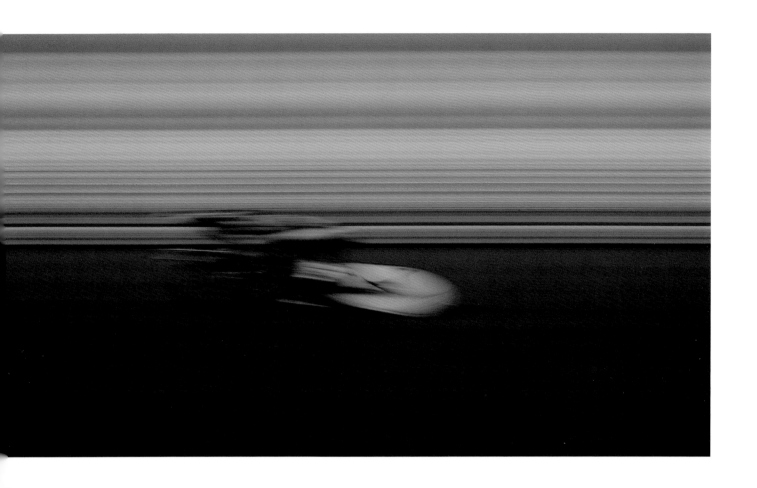

THE LEGS IN THE PORTALOO

A chance encounter at Goodwood

At the world championships at Goodwood in 1982, I stood just after the last corner on the final lap. Opposite me was the point at which Giuseppe Saronni made his final kick. I did not know that man could be so fast and so devastating, all in one pedal stroke. Astonishing.

Before the race began I had walked into a Portaloo, that very English of outdoor institutions. As I took a leak, I heard the clacking of shoe cleats on the lino and Italian voices behind me. I was aware of the pungent smell of continental liniment – a particular smell, mixing expensive cologne with embrocation. As I looked down, rearranging the bloo cubes in the pisser, all I could see next to me was a pair of immaculately shaved brown legs, perfectly folded white cotton ribbed socks and perforated calf-leather racing shoes. I really wanted to turn and stare but I froze and ran out to be greeted by the smell of fried onions and burgers. It was to be a day of contrasts.

Later that day I witnessed the sad parochial racism of the English spectators towards the riders from African nations. Their riders were a shambles, and they had terrible bikes, with long plastic tubes from bidon to handlebars wrapped around their frames like spaghetti. I presumed it was so they could drink and hang on simultaneously.

Some in the crowd had a dig at them for not being stylish, probably while wearing a Lycra balaclava or some foul purple club jersey (you know who you are) which they had worn in the open '25' that morning. Granted, the bidon spaghetti wasn't the closest thing to Italian style, but the ribbing coming from the Brits was a bit rich.

The legs in the Portaloo, I discovered belonged to Francesco Moser, the star of the Sanson team and the epitome of the glamour that surrounded the Italian squad

At the finish, Saronni was surrounded by police. I slipped through the cordon and bagged Beppe's autograph. I went home with both it and a fixed idea of what it is to be a real bike rider. And it did not involve anything British. The legs in the Portaloo, I discovered belonged to Francesco Moser, star of the Sanson team and the epitome of the glamour that surrounded the Italian squad.

Paradoxically, we English always had a peculiar affinity with Moser, partly because one of ours was his domestique. Big Dave Akam, the unlikely tester from the West Country (who was probably more familiar with the smell of Deep Heat, village halls and Portaloos than those Italian liniments) was employed to ride alongside Moser, mainly because he rode the same sized bike.

The encounter with Moser had a remarkable impression on me. The trade cap perched high on the head, the woollen shorts, the neat embroidered logos – they did it all with so much style. It was their era, too – any of their team could have won that day, and it was the beginning of the end for the dominance of the Azzurri.

After my encounter in the loo, I was forever a Moser fan. He rode the toughest races, and like me he was a big rider. But he also had that certain something that the rest of the peloton struggled with: even when he didn't win, he had class. All Moser fans will relish the film *A Sunday in Hell* as he rode all day in the dust and grime yet his world champion's jersey still managed to stay clean. But it was the Sanson kit that I remember best – the leather gloves, the Campagnolo logoed shorts. It was just all so right and was made for Moser.

Thereafter, we would sprint for signs on club runs, with the winner winning the rights to be Moser for the rest of the day. For me, he was the one and still is. He rode with the ultimate panache and was the last of the Italian style icons: never since has there been an Italian rider with as much class.

In my mind, he still holds the hour record. ◆

THE JOURNEY SO FAR
In conversation with Camille J McMillan

Give us a brief account of your cycling background.

I was seven when I first got on a bike. My old man, Rhett – he was born the same year that *Gone With the Wind* was released – was a keen club racer in the 50s and 60s and I picked up on that. He bought me an Elswick Hopper and by 14 I was racing, every minute of every day. In the winter cyclocross, in the summer road racing. Happiness for me as a kid was riding behind him on his motorbike, him pacing me. I was into speed. He was a big influence in my life, cycling was the place where we met.

Back then my dream was to win in pro racing. I was completely obsessed, riding all the time and winning a lot of races.

So what made you quit?

It was strange. I was 19 and won a race – and realised with a shock that I just didn't care. There was no feeling to it, no passion behind it. I stopped there and then and didn't pick a bike up for years: I went cold turkey, if you like, on the most powerful drug I knew.

Is that when you picked up a camera?

No – I moved to London, got a restaurant job in Soho and did the real drugs: out all the time, drink, women, whatever got thrown at me. At about 21 though I had a wake-up call. I took far too many drugs and woke up to what I was doing with my life.

So what happened next?

I'd always loved photography and knew what I wanted to say with a camera, so went to art school in London, then on to a degree at Central St. Martins.

Every year I went to the Good Friday meeting in London with the old man, and this time it was to take pictures of the madness there. There were no other photographers – no one was doing it back then. At that stage I was interested in graphic images: shapes and forms. Story-

telling came later, about 2001, when I got a Leica. Before then I'd been working digitally, shooting film then scanning it to strip it back down to the essentials. But the Leica changed that. I went back to film, and moved into narrative. Back then that was bad wookey! A dead thing that no one was doing.

And now?

It was hard at first but I started by using the Leica in the pub. Inhibitions were looser, and I learned how to get close up, how to deal with difficult lighting situations. You have to learn how to be part of what's going on and the camera has to be incidental to that.

So things were cool?

Yes. Very. I started taking a lot of racing pictures and got my bike out of the shed. Somehow shooting bike racing was my way of trying to understand my life before. All my generation – people I'd beaten! – were winning the Tour de France. What had I done? I woke up and joined the party again.

Around 2006 I was shooting a race in Surrey and saw a guy so enraged by puncturing that he threw his bike in a hedge. (I was too busy laughing to catch the shot.)

Later I spotted this very interesting company starting up, called Rapha, and a magazine called *Rouleur*, both doing my kind of thing. I went to see *Rouleur*, and the editor was the guy who'd thrown his bike in the hedge. I told him to give me a job or I'd expose him! I became Editor at Large. So just when I'd been shooting narrative photography and racing for a few years, these upstarts came along. It was just at the right time. I knew what I was talking about – I had the joint background of both an artist and a racer and the combination worked very well at that time. I worked with them for three years, but they went in a different direction in the end.   ▷

I knew what I was talking about – I had the joint background of both an artist and a racer and the combination worked very well at that time

◁ **Do you wish you'd carried on riding for a living, or are you glad to be behind the lens?**
I couldn't have done it: I just don't think I could ever do a job where I had to wear a uniform, and maybe too much too young?

You followed Team Sky at the beginning of their cycling journey. What was that like?
It was a great commission from *The Times*, following them for the Spring Classics. From the outset you could see the team was something else. They behaved so differently: stayed in 5-star hotels, came from a great track background – came to upset everyone! I could see with that much backing and fresh eyes they were going to make waves in a sport steeped in such history. I thought they were the sporting equivalent of New Labour. Agree or not, they were incredibly fresh and different.

But me, I liked all the tradition. Cycling as something akin to a religion. For that reason, ultimately theirs wasn't a story I was too interested in.

So what happened next?
I'd known John Herety since I was a kid. He's a great guy. I met him early on when he was talent spotting but I didn't want any of that team thing. But things go round and come back again and I met him later when he

was running the Rapha Condor Sharp pro cycling team. So I started shooting for them.

By then you'd done your first book *Le Métier* – whch is still regularly listed as one of the top ten classic cycling books of all time.
Is it? Hmm. Well, that's good.

I did *Le Métier* in 2008 with Michael Barry when he was in T-Mobile/HTC-Highroad. But I'd known him from school days. My old man was in the same cycling club as Barry's dad. At one stage I was bundled off to school in Canada – later expelled, you don't want to know – and he was there. Michael and his dad often stayed at our house in England.

Michael suggested the book – he wrote it and I shot it over two years. It was fabulous, great access, right up to sleeping in the same room as riders. I hope the book tells the real, hard story of all the seasons in a professional cyclist's life. Glamorous it's not.

How is *Circus* different from *Le Métier*?
It's a distillation of many years of shooting racing stories, from Grand Tours to small one-day events, and shot from the mechanic to the team owner. I edited out all the images shot on film, apart from one chapter on Six-Day races as I wanted to create a deliberately old-fashioned look. So it's all ▷

Above
Roubaix velodrome
The finish of the race the pro peloton fears the most – Paris-Roubaix; *Hell Of The North*. The velodrome is antiquated, odd, open, with concrete shower stalls. There is nothing appealing about them other than the hot water that flows from the steel shower heads.

Above
Pain and suffering
The old man, pictured, giving it the beans in some cyclocross event in 1968. Nothing gave him more pleasure than making the other competitors suffer. You can see the aggression in his face.

Opposite
Off the wall
Experiment with a warped mirror at a Spring Classic, shot for *Rouleur* magazine.

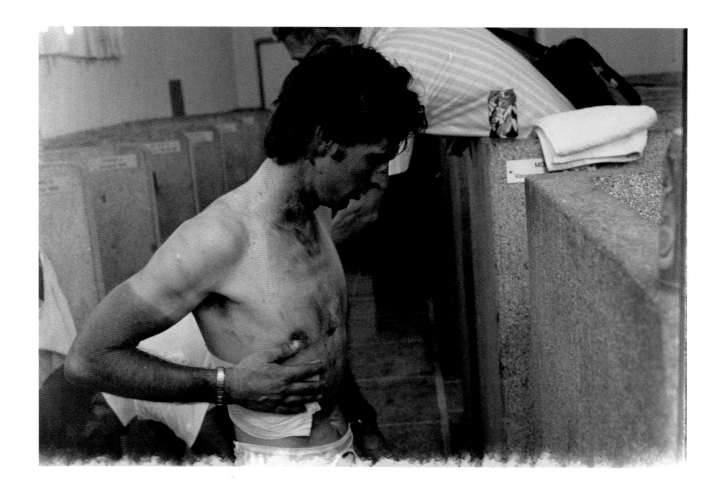

digital, images simply chosen from the stories I liked best with a kind of narrative sense that worked with that edit.

It was great looking back over so many years. And fascinating seeing the rise of Cav and Wiggins: both immense cyclists. Looking back at the shots I took of them at the 2007 Ghent 6-day races they look so young. Wiggins was mucking about with a towel, aping the Russian roulette scene from *The Deer Hunter* with his fingers for a laugh. I saw a lot of both of them in those early days: unpolished diamonds.

Cav was a rising star at T-Mobile. When Sky turned up he was noticed a lot more. But from the inside, seeing the rapid rise of these names was just a bit strange. The mass rise in the popularity of cycling was I think the result of a lot of influences coming together: the tube bombings in London, arguably, which coincided with the advent of the fixie culture. Then Rapha's arrival, plus Cav and Wiggins. I'm not sure cycling in Britain would have got so big without those things coming together all at the same time.

Those guys would have been big names in cycling, certainly. But the mass-cycling revolution perhaps would not have happened with them alone.

It's a subject for endless discussion.

How do you get the images you do – do you recce stages beforehand, say?
Sometimes I pop in and out of a race, taking what is there but yes, I'll bomb around trying to get a place that says 'here is where we are', or a great backdrop or good light. I'll work an area so I know what the angles are, and find alternatives so I can move at the last minute if the light changes.

Waiting for the peleton, I get excited. You can hear the helicopters coming... I'll still be moving around looking for the right spot, taking test shots. I love the pressure of knowing there are incoming cyclists and making decisions: should I be here, over there? When they arrive it's very physical – a wall of air hits you as they power past. But by then I'm in the camera.

Do you have imagery in mind before you arrive at a race?
No, it really all depends on the race. On the Tour de France say, you're responding all the time. If it's really windy for instance, you'd look at echelons. If it was brutally wet, you'd follow the soigneurs. Sometimes with the smaller races I'll have a story in mind.

Motos – the motorbikes that can follow the race – change things as they increase your access and make it easier to tell a story.

Roubaix showers
Each shower has a plaque etched with the race winner's name and the year he won. Some riders look for a shower with their hero's name on it. Others, like battered Servais Knaven here, who won in 2001, use their own stall. The orange flare on the image is from light getting into the camera. Luckily it was the last frame on the roll and I saved it.

Team time trial

The final Grand Tour of the 2010 season, the Vuelta a Espana, kicked off in Seville with an evening team time trial. It was incredible. Still very hot. And so fast. Here's team Sky going full gas, lit by team-car headlights.

How does working in the UK on the Tour of Britain differ from the continental races you've covered?

Everything's on the wrong side of the road! It's a very different vibe. It's a bit like a farmers' market, when people come over from Europe for a spell to sell their goods. A smaller scale of course, but getting bigger each year. Inside the cordon it's just the same as the Grand Tours though.

During the races do you find you're sometimes at odds with the other photographers, given your 'alternative' approach to how you photograph cycling?

I have no problem with traditional sports photographers, not at all. They are doing their thing, I'm doing mine: that's fine. But I've no truck with opportunist photographers, coming along just because it's cool. A lot come along with no vision, no point of view, and don't know what they are doing. Or they're just trying to make money. There's more to cycling than the 'epic shot' – I get irritated when the same old sh*t is trotted out – solo rider going over the mountain pass, yada yada...

There are some great photographers out there still. But I have a feeling their kind of story telling is being muscled out by the winning-line promo shot.

What's been your favourite race?

Got to be the Tour de France. But it depends... the best adventures were perhaps on the Tour of Britain, working with Tom Southam. (But what goes on the tour stays on the tour!)

Paris-Roubaix is always good. Great shots of belting across pavé, the dust, the pain. But riding my own motorbike to cover the Tour de France was an amazing trip.

What next for Camille, the image maker?

More bike racing but perhaps portraits, more as a photo journalist. I'd also like to edit a magazine and to commission stuff. I like other people's work. But my magazine would be more *Fear and Loathing*. Journalists should push against the sanitisation of cycling, against all that corporate massaging and faux transparency. Go tell some real stories. Go undercover into the UCI as photo journalist. Be more Gonzo.

That. And getting back on the bike... ◆

Yesterday coming up a hill – they were coming up a cobbled rise – you could hear the clatter of the bikes. You couldn't see the bikes. You could see the lead cars, but you could hear the clattering of the bikes, and you could hear the rush and the excitement of the crowd. You could feel it. And as they came past it raised the hairs on my head as they thundered past. It's just the feeling of it. There's a definite fear. You can smell it. Yeah – it's exciting.

Ardennes classics feed station

One of my favourites.

KODAK 160NC-2

21A

IT'S THE REAL THING
Missouri: fast cars, quick thinking

I land in Kansas City, excited. I have never been to the Midwest. I'm following this bike rider for a year, but I have been stuck in a studio shooting crap for what feels like months. I am in a twisted half-mind state, jet lagged, and unsure of how many Stillnox with gin and tonics I had on the flight over. The dreams are leaching into the daylight, the boundaries of waking and sleep are blurred and before the heat has hit me, I'm pulling out of the most automated car hire place in the most automated car I have ever been in. I pull straight onto the interstate and head out towards St Louis. It's easy, all is automated and I'm not in Kansas no more.

The Dodge's big motor was strong, and roared from a standstill. It's what I imagined a big 'yank tank' would do. I was pleased. A real big one, just like I had ordered online back in the UK. Air-conditioned, silent power. I was in a hurry to meet up with the race. I am two days late.

For what feels like an eternity, I go down the interstate passing the occasional sign for Route 66. Eventually I take a right turn signed Ozarks. The road was big but twisty, taking me through place names that are familiar, very old English names, on into the Ozark mountains. I pass trailer home after trailer home – each with a huge car on bricks in front of it. The clichés stack up on each other. Preconceived banjos twang: I'm wondering where *Deliverance* was shot.

Eventually I reach a crossroads, an unusual event outside of a town. The ex gas station at the junction has the full Americana faded glory; the kind of place where people like to take black and white pictures of peeling paint. There is even old neon sign pointing to an erased motel; dead, old signage. I start to think about *Psycho,* and how Anthony Perkins had died from complications arising from AIDS a long, long time before.

Tour of Missouri, 2008
Chasing the peloton, on the back of a moto.

Yes – this was a crossroads, Blues tunes filling my head... this is a trip with tunes.

I wanted to do the ice cold drink machine thing. Pull up, put a dime in the slot, get out a glass bottle of the fizzy black sh*t. Not a chance. I have to go in for my cola.

It was dark, and smelly... an amateur taxidermist's shop. The banjo really had started to twang and before I had time to turn and run, Steve had already said 'Hi'. I was trapped.

As my eyes grew accustomed to the dark, I looked down at row upon row of arrow heads. Large, small, pretty, fearsome objects, wonderful stone objects... I'm transfixed by them and I could not remember why I was there. Whiskey? Maybe that was the way to go, but I'm clutching at straws... I remember a grim Bourbon experience, so I settled on a packet of red Marlboro – spending my first American dollars. Fumbling, and looking for reason to speak, I finally said I was looking for a bike race that comes this way. Steve said, 'yes Sir, it passes here in a hour'. Imagine a banjo string snapping. So the conversation starts. Steve can see I'm uneasy – I think he knows that I am thinking about the duelling banjos. Trying to put me at ease, he tells me he has travelled.

'Cool Steve, where?'

'With the Army. Iraq'. Another banjo string snaps. I start to open them Marlboro.

'NO! Not in here', says Steve 'Mom's on the oxygen now, so it's a little dangerous'. Steve and I go outside and smoke. We talk about his Mom's oxygen and the Native Americans. Steve spends his days hunting and stuffing deer heads, smoking or selling Marlboros. He hunts with a bow and arrow because he wants to connect with the Native Americans. He collects the old arrow heads he finds. I feel he will do this until the oxygen gets *him.*

As we are talking I keep returning to his words 'mom's on the oxygen now' Is he some kind of existential genius? ▷

I run towards the road. Fast decision time, the moment I live and breathe for, the moments I love: the bend before the finish – or try to get through the crowd? I go for the bend. I can see the race approaching. I put a new roll into the Leica as I run

◁ **The race passes in silence,** and no comments are made, I get two frames and the roll of film is finished. As the race passes a truck pulls in. It's Steve's friend, all swagger and brown baseball cap. I tell the guys I need to get to the finish. I'm informed there is no way of getting to the finish town before the race gets there – but Steve's friend says he coud give it a go.

I shake Steve's hand and get in the car. Steve points to follow his friend down an unremarkable road. Mom is waving from the porch at the back of the shop while attached to her oxygen tank.

I follow Steve's friend, and my Dodge is appalling. This big beast of a car is made for straight lines, for pulling away from traffic lights, stopping and repeating. We leave the paved road and hit gravel. Dust billows from the truck in front and the back end of my Dodge drifts out. This guy in front is motoring and my Sat-Nav has nothing to show but an arrow. We are on the dirt roads somewhere in Missouri. I think about the *Dukes of Hazzard*, and put my foot down. I push up to the truck in front. F*ck it! F*ck the car hire deposit – lets go! For the next hour we burn way too much gas, drift the bends and destroy the car's paint work.

It ends with a nothing; a bounce into a car park in a small town. There is a crowd at one side of the car park. I have been delivered to the finish of the day's stage! We quickly exchange a few 'dudes' and 'awesomes', and I run towards the road. Fast decision time, the moment I live and breathe for, the moments I love: the bend before the finish – or try to get through the crowd? I go for the bend. I can see the race approaching. I put a new roll into the Leica as I run. I reach the kerb, put the camera to my eye and take a picture of the approaching race. There is a lone rider soloing to victory. The luck! It's the rider I am following for the year, Michael Barry, his only professional win in his long career. ◆

Tour of Missouri, 2008
Stage 4, Michael Barry rounds the final bend – driving on for a fine solo win.

Empire Pool Indoor Arena
Wembley
16th-21st September 1977   40p

SIX-DAYS
It's not just about the cycling

Smoky, beery with the sound of the Derny's two-stroke engines so loud the cheers were swamped by them and *Popcorn* by Hot Butter smashed out over the top. That's where I saw Eddy Merckx and Patric Sercu race. That's where I got a taste for speed and showmanship: it was at the Skol 6 in Wembley Arena as a 10-year-old-boy.

After the races I would fall asleep in the back of the old man's VW Variant, driving through the late winter night, listening to the rear-engined motor and sometimes throwing up the hot dogs I'd wolfed at the race.

30-something years later I know the original Gershon Kingsley version of *Popcorn* and I know what Six-day races were. And that they are – just about – surviving.

After Patric Sercu – eleven times winner and now the ring-master and owner of the Six-days – gave me the nod and I walked into the cabin area of one of those races. I was ten again, ecstatic.

This section is a celebration of a type of racing that feels almost gone... and I got the most fabulous days of it as a boy.

The many different Six-day races here were all shot on film using either a Leica, a Hasselblad or my Mamiya Press 6x9. For me they felt the correct tools and retro medium to use to express this dying outpost of cycling, and my childhood excitement.

Opposite

Transvestite spectator
2007, Bremen. It was ladies' night. There are a lot of dockers there. There are a few rough trannies too.

Zabel's cabin

Milram sell milk. Zabel's in his lair, which he'll
share with a teammate for the week.
They have a little privacy curtain, so they can
p*ss in their bucket or get a massage or
just try to get away from the noise. It's very
cell-like. Zabel's cabin was next to the
finish line, so the podium girls tend to hang
around there too.

In the workshop
Roberto Chiappa inspects a chain at the track league at the
Amsterdam Six. Two worlds coexist. Hard work and hard
partying. Just beyond him people are wining and dining in
the track-centre restaurant.

Sponsors' names at the Amsterdam Six

The Amsterdam Six is very civilised. There's only people dining in the
middle. Unlike Ghent, which is a pig pen. It's the opposite of Ghent.

Starter pistol

I'm not sure what that thing is on the right. It's probably a mic of some sort. Smoking's been banned now, though. Six was all about late night, smoking and drinking. And discarded weaponry. This is normally where Patrick Sercu who owns the Six-day stands. He rules with an iron fist in an iron glove. Holding a gun.

Above

Iljo Keisse

The Belgian is getting a rub while talking to
Dutch teammate Danny Stam. Keisse
has won the Six Days of Ghent six times.

Opposite top

Marvulli waits

That's Franco Marvulli sitting down, and
I think that's his soigneur. There's a
devil or something going on and he's bored.
The pit in Ghent is sunken.

Opposite below

Roberto Chiappa

Roberto has the biggest legs I've ever seen.

Overleaf

The Madison

The riders are setting themselves up for a
hand-sling. I used a 12mm lens for this
shot and had to stand like Charlie Chaplin
to stop getting my feet in the frame. I had to
pan to keep the focus and I shot it wide open...
I knew I'd be able to capture the chaos
through the sort of controlled distortion.
My granny went to school with Chaplin.

The hand-sling

There's a real mixture of kit, from old steel to monocoque carbon in a velodrome. The kit doesn't wear out like on the road. No diesel, oil, salt or grime. Clean machines. They race from about seven in the evening until they've sold all the beer at about two or three in the morning.

The final lap, Bremen It's the final night and it's the bell for the final sprint of the Six-day. Zabel, the local hero riding for Team Milram, needs to win the final sprint to win...

...and he wins by half a wheel. The winners, Erik Zabel and Swiss rider, Bruno Risi. The podium. The glory. The confetti.

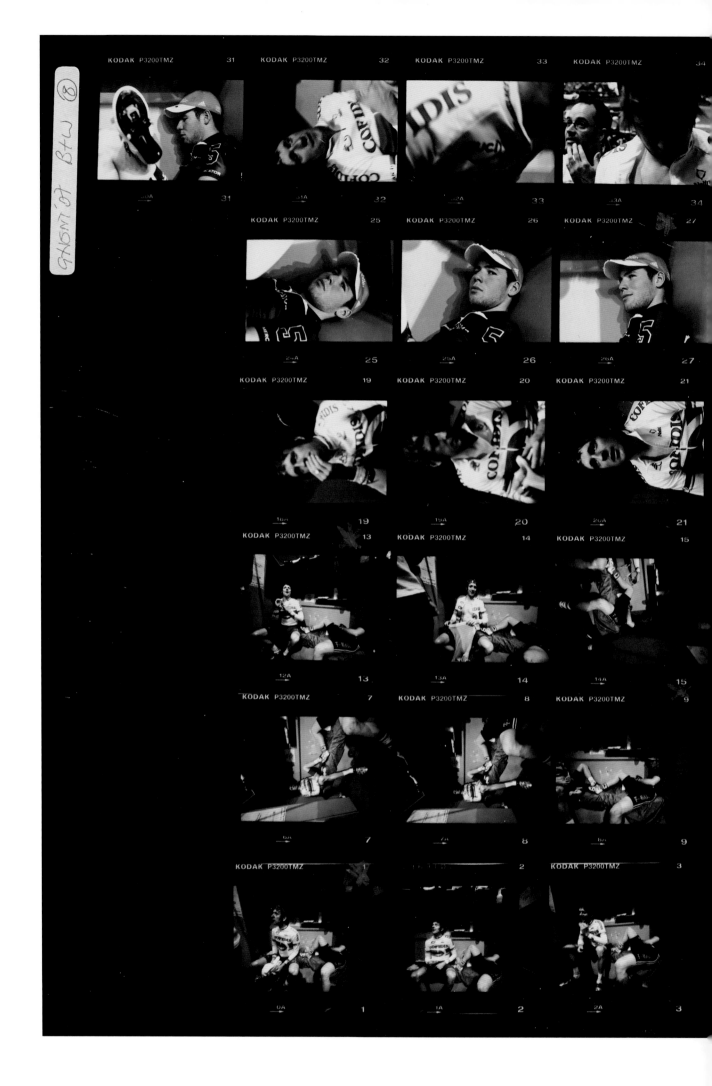

Leica contact sheet #1
A young Bradley Wiggins, and partner
Mark Cavendish, then riding for
Cofidis and T-Mobile respectively, pictured
in their 'cabin', in the middle of the
velodrome, during the 2007 Six Days of
Ghent event. When I shot this roll of film,
they were in 12th place and 10 laps behind.
The mood was tense.

Six Days of Ghent – Brits in the pit

The atmosphere inside the Ghent's famous
't Kuipke building was buzzing. It smelt
of hotdogs, burgers, beer and embrocation.

In the middle of the track there was
a party going on. But in one rider cabin the
mood was dark.

The word going around the cabins that
night was that other riders were p*ssed off
with Wiggins. Wiggins, in turn, was p*ssed
off with his partner.

Brad's partner that evening was a young
Mark Cavendish – and he was off the pace.
Apparently he'd had a heavy two weeks
of off-season and while Wiggins was laying
down the speed – fast times – making
the racing super-hard for the other racers,
Cav was dropping laps.

Back then, to get to the riders' cabins you
had to get through the tightly packed track
centre; a mosh pit full of smoking, drunk,
noisy Belgians and non-smoking, drunk Brits.
Going into their tiny dark cabin I could
instantly feel the atmosphere was not good.
In the right corner Cav, in the left Brad.
It felt like the pause between rounds of
a boxing match.

I started shooting them with my
Hasselblad, but it came apart in my hands
after a roll or two. The top focus loop-thing
fell apart... it instantly broke the atmosphere.
Cav and Wiggins joked about my
unprofessionalism. I pulled out my old Leica
and continued to shoot. These contact
sheets are from both cameras.

We had a banter, during which Wiggins
revealed one of his big talents. He is a master
mimic. Quite extraordinary to see. I have
seen him impersonate Ian Curtis since, but
on this night he was De Niro, in *Deer Hunter*.

Hasselblad contact sheet
Ghent velodrome, 2007.

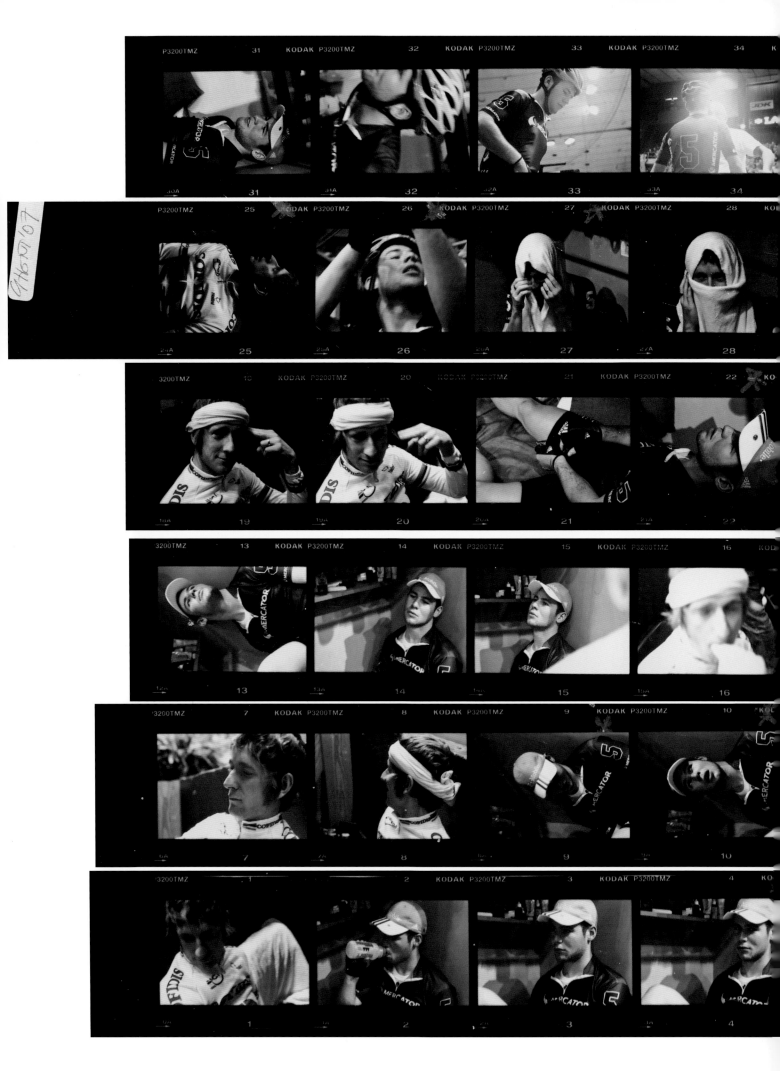

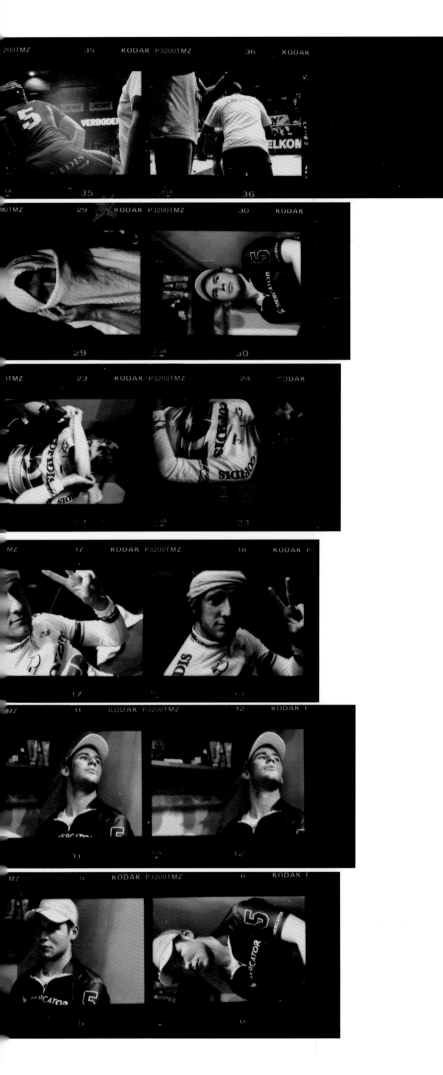

Leica contact sheet #2

The boys cheered up when my Hasselblad broke after shooting just one roll, and Wiggins is seen here doing his *Deer Hunter* impression. Years later, Cav ribbed me again for shooting digitally.

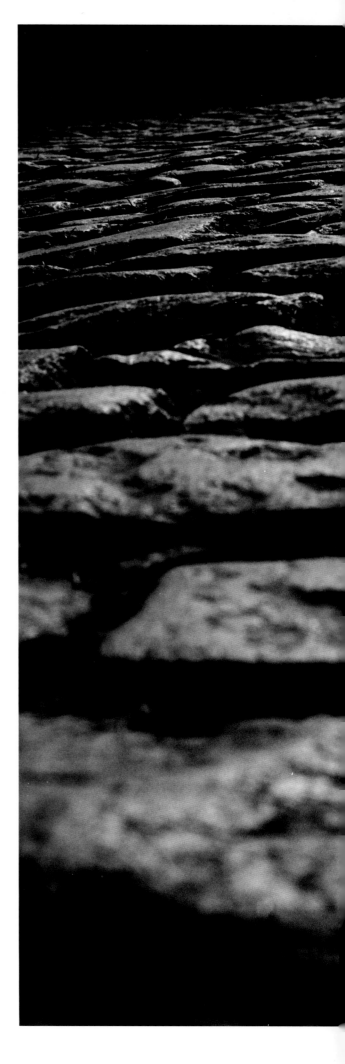

THE SPRING CLASSICS
Cycling's greatest one-day races

We were on a road trip in a yellow Austin Allegro. Northern France was a pretty thing. I marvelled at its difference as the grown-ups moaned that petrol would soon be £1 a gallon. We were going over the water on a hovercraft to the land of bike racing. As passengers suffered on the rough hovercraft crossing, I was becoming full-tilt excited.

We camped, and at our campsite there was a friend of a friend of the old man's in a camper. He was a photographer called Graham, working for *Cycling Weekly* and breaking into the continental scene.

I was taken with his life, his kit, how he lived: even then I had interest in the image. In a way Graham Watson must have had an influence on my photographic journey, perhaps not in the same way as Alexander Rodchenko, Josef Koudelka or Leni Riefenstahl. But there it is, Graham Watson's influence on my life, my career path.

Since then I have headed to France and Belgium to those Spring Classics in more than a Hillman Avenger: chasing the action in furious Subaru Imprezas, super-fast Audis, a magazine editor's Yaris, BMW cars and bikes... Best of all, smashing over the pavé of the Paris-Roubaix on a KTM. That's a trip that still makes many puke, but for me it's always a buzz. Nearly as good as watching Jan Raas hammering the others into submission in his woolly Ti Raleigh kit.

Classic indeed.

Paris-Roubaix
Queen of the Classics. Hell of the North. This is the race that can define a career or end one. And of the twenty seven sections of brutal pavé, the Arenberg Forest is the section that riders fear the most.

This page

Dwars door Vlaanderen, 2012

Sky's classics team staff. Bus drivers, soigneurs and directeurs sportif all having breakfast before the off. The mechanics are loading up the team cars outside.

Overleaf, clockwise from top left

Morning light

You don't see scenes like this very often. You don't really see pro cyclists in these places. Get to know that it's just like getting ready for work. They're like sales executives in a Travel Tavern.

TV

Mathew Hayman and Jeremy Hunt were rooming together. There are screens everywhere with Sky. The TV is always on. Some Belgian nonsense on it.

Hotel hallway

That's Michael Barry talking to someone in the door. I like the light on the right. It was a great hotel. It almost bankrupted me staying there.

Almost ready

I like this one because it looks like Jeremy Hunt's going to walk into a wall.

This page

Omloop Het Volk

The opening event on the Belgian cycling
calendar and often characterized by
cold weather. Mr Handsome here gets his
first public massage of the season.
In a transit van.

Overleaf

Kuurne–Brussels–Kuurne

I found myself in this quiet car park. There's
only a few team cars and a couple of buses
in there. And a horsebox. What with the
gambling and the way some of the riders are
treated, they might as well be horses.

Above

Omloop Het Nieuwsblad

You see funny little things if you look carefully at the start line. Intimacy can take many forms. In this instance, a rider from another team is allowed to steady himself on a rival's brake hood.

Opposite

Omloop Het Nieuwsblad

Tension starts to mount at the start line. This rider lost his race numbers and had to resort to making his own. He probably got a fine.

Overleaf

Kuurne–Brussels–Kuurne

He's going through the Latvian's pockets. Looking for something... probably to twiddle his radio.

Ronde van Vlaanderen

Early pavé. The first bend in one of the early sectors. Some of the
pavé is really smooth, and it's been re-done so many times. It's almost
like a shopping precinct. The whole of Flanders is very gentrified.
I read somewhere that American post-war suburbia is based on
Belgium. It's the most densely populated country. You never seem to
leave an urban environment. A whole country of suburbia, apart
from Wallonia, which is nice.

Overleaf

La Flèche Wallonne

It's rare in the Sping Classics to see the peloton strung out from
a distance. I don't usually take this kind of shot. This is a race
more suited to the specialist power climber who excels at producing
that final effort on the 1.3km Mur de Huy.

Opposite top
Liège–Bastogne–Liège, 2011
Passing the bottle. That's a commissaire
looking on, making sure he's not sticky
bottling. See his smirk… and the rider looking
straight ahead. 'Not I, guv…'

Opposite below
Liège–Bastogne–Liège, 2011
Just move the whole living room suite
on to the side of the road why don't you.
We're not in Flanders now, Dorothy –
Wallonia is a lot rougher.

Above
Dwars door Vlaanderen , 2011
Exchange. I love the way Juan Antonio
Flecha is so dainty. It's so fast, but you can
see his soigneur, Stefan's focus. The eye
contact is interesting – they're both fixated
on the bottle and the hands. Behind, there's
Geraint Thomas following Fabian Cancellara.
There's a lot of big hitters in this picture.

Overleaf
Ronde van Vlaanderen, 2011
Dark skies rolling in – almost as fast as the
peloton. This is when the pavé gets tricky!

Paris-Roubaix, 2011

The chasing pack. This is one of the final sections of cobbles on this 250km race, legendary for its brutal stretches of pavé. Eventual winner Johan Vansummeren has just gone through. My moto's on the grass verge there. I've stepped out on to the road. Mathew Hayman is working his ass off – it's brutally hard work over this kind of terrain – for the whole peloton. Some pro cyclists dismiss it because of its difficult conditions.

Above

Paris-Roubaix

The pack crashes. I'm standing on the back
of the moto, which is still parked, and
there's this crash. BMC thought I'd caused it,
but I was on the moto, and other photos
showed that we were safely on the verge.

Opposite above

Crash on the cobbles

It's all so ungainly. Martin Reimer and Romain
Zingle. It's such a slow crash, they just got
themselves all tangled up. There's a lot of slow
crashes that just cause irritation rather than
damage. I love awkward moments in cycling.

Opposite below

A Saur-Sojasun rider crashes

Whoops! Another rider hits the deck as the
pace increases towards the race climax.

Previous page

Ronde van Vlaanderen

Single-day road specialist, Tom Boonen, hugs
the barriers during this spring classic.

Opposite top

It's all mashed up

That rider was caught in no man's land
between the breakaway and the pack.

Opposite bottom

Ronde van Vlaanderen

Chasing. Always chasing – or being chased.

Overleaf

Paris-Roubaix

The Arenberg! Here I'm p*ssing off someone,
on the right, with a huge great lens 'cos I'm
in his picture. That's the legendary Arenberg
cobbles. But it was a bit of a damp squib.
Or a dry squib. It wasn't dangerous, it was
just fast. More image-makers there than you
could shake a stick at, almost more than fans.

Omloop Het Volk, 2009

This was the first time I saw the peloton that year, coming in race mode. It was a really fast descent, and a sweeping right-hander. They were really close in this one and the lens is very wide. In the middle of it, I thought, 'Here we are, back again. The season's started.' I like Wouter Weylandt, nearest the camera, and that house in particular. It's been chopped in half. I think a tank went through it.

Overleaf

Ronde van Vlaanderen

The hype of last year's race was that Fabian Cancellara was going to destroy everyone. I saw someone in the crowd that day holding a sign that said 'Fabian please have mercy'. It's because he destroyed everyone in the E3-Harelbeke – and of course there were the outlandish 'motor' rumours the year before.

La Flèche Wallonne

This is the final dig before the original finish line – up the Mur de Huy. I saw these girls on a roof; the perfect vantage point to shoot from, and persuaded them to let me join them. They're loving it. Their boyfriends were downstairs watching football on the TV – they couldn't care less what was happening in the race.

Overleaf
Mur de Huy
Phillipe Gilbert kills it!

Previous page
Liège–Bastogne–Liège, 2011
The winner. It's such a shame about the
bad light. That wall of cameras is what
faces the riders at each finish. This is the
second row of photographers waiting for
their money shots. With this win Philip Gilbert
scored a rare hat-trick of victories in the
tough Ardennes classics comprising this,
Flèche Wallonne and the Amstel Gold race.

Left
Liège–Bastogne–Liège
Tejay Van Garderen – total exhaustion.
In his black shirt, the soigneur looks like a
military guard: you don't want to mess with
him. That's a seething mass of soigneurs,
riders and fans at the finish line. They couldn't
be contained.

Above

Kuurne–Brussels–Kuurne, 2009

Tom Boonen took it off Bernhard Eisel.
It was his first big win of the season.
I don't usually hang around for the winner,
I was just in the right place at the right
time. Which is unusual for me. Normally
I'm in the right place at the wrong time.

Opposite top

La Flèche Wallonne

The press want their pound of flesh,
and he has to give them the time. It's all
part of the game. There's no hiding.

Opposite below

Ghent–Wevelgem

Look at the crowd looking on, they're
merciless. Does Ian Stannard and his fellow
riders think it's intrusive? I don't think so.

Three Days of De Panne
At the end of the race Sky rider
Chris Sutton pokes his head out of the team
bus, *Shining*-style.

Previous page and this spread
Tour de Suisse
Michael Barry. Shagged. Post-race
pain, suffering and tan lines.

Dwars door Vlaanderen

Sky Directeur Sportif Steven de Jongh,
seated, to his left is Servais Knaven, and on
the right Sky's Head of Operations,
Carsten Jeppesen, discuss a day's racing.
The dark room and lighting give this portrait
a dramatic feel.

The massage

"I look dead in that picture," Hunt said
to me when he saw it.
There is something of the cadaver about it.

SUMMER
It's all about the Tour de France

The tour was it, the motherload. I never saw it as a kid other than through the eyes of TV. But I knew I wanted to be in it. Summers were punctuated with racing three days a week and watching the Channel 4 coverage.

As a kid the pro racing was fuelled with amphetamines, heroic rides, suicidal breaks. It was very different to the next age of EPO and race radio. If I had stepped over into the Pro world I guess I would have walked into the new dawn of EPO and riders' sudden death from heart failure. This new age never held my focus or excitement. The boring eras of individuals dominating TdF after TdF. The Armstrong years just left me cold. Back then I never found myself wanting to photograph Armstrong: I've got about two shots of him. Now I know why.

I got back in the groove in 2006. It's where I found more of cycling than I imagined. It's where I first started to think, this world of the Tour is bonkers! Getting up at sparrow's fart o'clock, criss-crossing France after the riders for thousands of kilometres on my moto, sweltering in the heat under my leathers. Sometimes I'd be so tired I'd get to a campsite in the evening and just sleep next to the bike, still in my gear. After a while I thought the leathers could have driven the bike themselves. If only I could teach them to take pictures too.

But I had it easy. Riders rolling over the line, ashen and grey like corpses under the sweat and suntan. The craziness of the hot, crowded mountain stages: Mont Ventoux, Alpe d'Huez. Preceding them once up Ventoux I wore my horn out beeping at the crowds.

It's a mad circus.

'Cos it's tradition
The lion was actually the mascot of longtime Tour de France title sponsor Crédit Lyonnais. According to French sports magazine *L'Équipe*, the bank has been handing out the fluffy lions at the Tour since 1987.

Glossy box

Commentators in their control booth,
looking more like a fairground attraction, get
ready for the day's racing.

This page

Garmin Cervélo tour bus

David Zabriskie gets his race face on.

Opposite

Garmin Cervélo tour bus

Belgian cyclist, Johan Vansummeren, finds time for one more caffeine hit before setting off. He's patched up from hitting the deck during the previous day's race shenanigans.

Overleaf

Focussed at the start

Canadian cyclist, Ryder Hesjedal makes final adjustments – all under intense scrutiny from race photographers.

Previous page
The prologue
Dan Martin flies off the start ramp.

Above
Tour de France, various stages
The fans gather. Some have been waiting
hours... others days.

Opposite
Corsica
Wearing leathers I waited here all day in
40 degree heat and got talking with
a family. Afterwards, I went for a naked
swim with the grand-dad in a nearby
pool of icy meltwater.

Overleaf
Tour crucifixion
Natives gather on the skyline... and is
that a mountain top sacrifice of a child on
that Tour summit marker?

Previous page
Tour clown
Clowns are meant to be entertaining, but
this one looked pretty sinister – exaggerated
by the dead flies caught in his yellow wig.

Above and opposite
Le peloton est arrivé
The freebies – caps, Haribos, key fobs, cakes,
anything – thrown to the crowds from
the noisy publicity caravan preceding the
race are all part of the scene.

Tour de France
Road Graffitti. Fun Pants. I've no idea...

Opposite top
Mont Ventoux
Check out the dude on the exercise bike.

Opposite bottom
Mont Ventoux
Waiting. Waiting. Tour campervans are
ever-present in the mountains.

Following pages
The mountains
p136-137: Lead riders competing for the
general classification crest the Col de la
Colombière to waiting soigneurs with bidons.
Cadel Evans is battling to stay on
the wheel of race leader, Bradley Wiggins.

p138-139: And then the 'bus'; those
riders who battle to finish stages that don't
suit them. That said, for a 'non-climber',
Mark Cavendish would still smash any
amateur cyclist. Here he clips off the front
for his bidon.

p140-141: Over the summit, the French
housewives' favourite, Tommy Voeckler,
momentarily lets go of his bars as he adjusts
position for a high-speed descent.

FROOME DOP

JAJA REVIE

G UNE ION!

MIMI ♥ AURÉ — MÉLA
CHELSEA — MARGO — NOA

IDUL AARON ♥ KARLOS

Heading for 100kph
Tommy Voeckler hooning down to Bagnères
de Luchon to win the stage in 2012.
Shooting at 1/64000th of a second freezes
the spokes. One shot, no motor wind.

Overleaf
Clipping the apex
Going full gas, the peloton hits the outskirts
of Chalabre, riders close enough to smell
the rosé on the breath of the spectators.

p152-153 **L'Arrivée**
Fans, gendarmes, media and Tour staffers
get set for the riders at Foix in 2012. In the
distance Stage 14 winner, Spain's Luis Léon
Sanchez, approaches the finish line.

It's all politics President François Hollande, above, appears at the finish line. It's all hand shakes and back slaps, with little apparent interest in the race itself.

Dan Martin wins the stage, dignitaries still pre-occupied with their mobile phones. Below, is he texting the wife or checking the race results?

Stage finish – 2012

It's all over. Phillipe Gilbert is escorted back
to his bus by his soigneur. From his face,
he didn't get he result he was hoping for.

Above and opposite

Post stage rituals

The media scrum descends as soon as
sweat-soaked riders finish a stage.
Even after Peter Sagan, *right*, has been
presented with his new green jersey,
the media demands continue.

Individual time trial, 2012

The toll. Dave Millar is a mess at the end of his 53km individual time trial, coughing his guts out after giving it his all. Many riders puke with the effort after finishing a time trial – 'the race of truth'.

All images

On the Champs-Élysées

It may be the most famous race finish in world sport, but the road surface is shocking. But it didn't stop Cavendish winning – wearing his favourite jersey – in 2012. The elation of finishing Le Tour is matched by the deflation of ending the 'Grand Boucle' for another year.

Overleaf

Get me outta here

At the race end, riders just want to get out, showered and away. Here one rider takes a short cut over the barriers to get to the champagne on the team bus...

AUTUMN
The Tour of Britain

I remember it as a very small boy in the Seventies when it
was with a different organisation. (The history of the
Tour of Britain is a complex thing.) The race came past the
house, fast and glinting in the sun, our house high
above the race. Later, watching *Jim'll Fix It* on telly, the old
man told me Jimmy Savile rode it once, and was a pro
bike rider! It made an impression.

Later on in the Eighties I bunked off school and rode out
30 miles to watch the Tour of Britain and saw the USSR
on their Colnagos. It was the longest I had ridden on my
own at that age. I was hooked on bike racing.

Many years later I followed the ToB on a number of
ocassions, I loved its Britishness. It was small and
intimate at the beginning. Over the years it has become
a behemoth like all of British cycling.

It was always the Autumn race for me: it had all the
ingredients of a continental race, with its team buses, team
cars and glamorous riders. But it had small teams too, their
riders changing out of race kit, roadside, in a town square.
I liked that, the story was the same as any other race, but
one could get close to it all. Back then, riders used to drink
a beer after a stage, chat to fans, no pressure.

Now it's on to the team bus and off to the sanctuary
of a five-star hotel and 'media opportunities' with the stars:
big bucks, marginal gains.

SANDON
PARISH

SANDON	¼	STONE	4
WESTON	2¾	NEWCASTLE	12½
RUGELEY	10½		
LICHFIELD	18		
LONDON	137		

This page
Tour bus
Rapha Condor rider, Tom Southam,
contemplating the work ahead in the
tranquillity of the team motor home.

Opposite
The glamour of it all
Even the amateurs will recognise this little
scene. The necessary pre race ritual...

The Sky team bus
Affectionately known as the 'Death Star'.
The crowds are always drawn to it,
and mingle waiting to glimpse the stars.

Cav. Lord of the Manor.

I asked him if I could use this photo – he said
"No problem, as long you can't see my c*ck."
He looks like he's thinking about something.

Pub peloton
Rapha Condor rider, Tom Southam, sits
on the wheel of 2009 Italian Road Race
Champion, Filippo Pozzato.

Overleaf
Up on the moor
A very British landscape. The race was
strung well out.

Above
Binned it
Andy Tennant has left his bike in a bush.
Here, he's coming to terms with the
consequences. He made it back on.

Opposite top
Yarrow Water
Nice landscape. Bit of water, bit of sky, bit of
Team Sky, bit of peloton.

Opposite below
Border crossing
Dark skies coming into England over the
border. The procession. Bandit country,
no spectators. The weather was grim – the
next day's stage was abandoned. Team Sky
were giving it some welly. They had
a miserable week though. The chopper looks
like a fly on my lens.

Overleaf
Pushing on
The Team Columbia-HTC, working for
Edvald Boason Hagen in 2009 – were
keeping the pace high – and the peloton
strung out.

Full gas

That was 4k to go, maybe less. They were
going for it. We had to open up to stay
ahead. When you're on the moto you have to
jam your leg in to keep straight. Standing on
the pegs. If the rider accelerates he'll often
put his arm back to stop you falling off.

Overleaf

The peloton

An echelon is forming and that's not the
arrow to follow. The peloton are
coming towards me. They own the road.

Both images

View from the team car

I'm in the back seat of the Team Sky car. That's
a breakaway that's not working, so they say
they want a drink, but actually just complain
and bitch about the other riders in the break.

Overleaf

Incoming

I hadn't taken my rain kit with me
as I thought it was going to be dry.
I was wearing jeans.

Above
Thor
Teammate, Dan Lloyd, was helping his boss,
and World Champion, Thor Hushovd in 2011.
It was windy. And wet. Revolting.
Not good weather for photographers.

Opposite
Cats and dogs
It was miserable on the moto.
I like the garden furniture. Good pictures
clump together. The doctor's put his roof up.

Overleaf
Caerphilly Mountain
Jonathan Tiernan-Locke moved into the
overall lead of the Tour of Britain on
stage six in 2012 after launching an attack on
the decisive climb.

Cav. Sprinter. Climber

Seeing Cav, wearing his World Champion's
rainbow jersey on Caerphilly Mountain in
2012, felt like being in continental Europe.
Incredible buzz. And yet very British.

Above

Hard as nails

I was on the moto at this point. I love Geraint
Thomas because he's a hard Welshman.
He's hard as nails. I like that picture
also because there's a big granite wall, like
a coalface. Dark Satanic Mill Street.

Opposite top

London

That's my moto waiting for me down there
while I was up on the bridge barging
tourists out of the way. I like the wire here –
a bit of left-over Christmas.

Opposite bottom

Job done

Matthew Hayman is finished for the day and
is spat out the back as the peloton
accelerates away in search of the breakaway.

Overleaf

Penultimate bend

After his 2011 stage win in London, Cav said:
'I didn't want to take too many risks today
with the Worlds coming up. It was a wet
finish and I saw [Ben] Swift lose his wheel on
the second last corner so I backed off on the
last corner and ended up 20 metres behind
coming out of it. I thought I was too far back
to get it but I went for it anyway and I came
through on the line'.

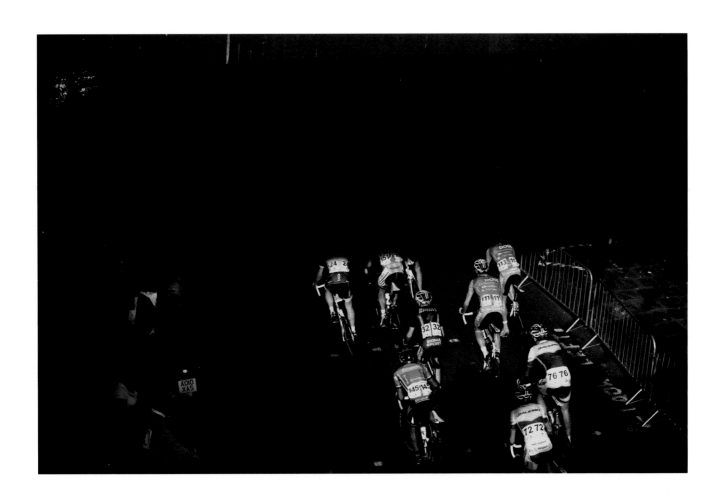

Previous page

Another win for Team Columbia-HTC.

There ws no stopping Edvald Boasson Hagen
in the 2009 edition of the race.
The fast Norwegian won four stages.

Opposite above

Kristian House is still looking ruined

The smaller team's vans are in a back street,
hidden away. While the big glory
buses are just off the main thoroughfare.

Opposite below

Final stage – in Guildford, 2012.

It just shows how 'in the street it is' for
the smaller teams. They just get on with it.
No team buses, spectators walking by –
looking at their bits.

It's over
Jeremy Hunt's last stage of his final race as a
professional. I spoke to Jez after the race
and asked if that was a tear rolling down his
face... I cannot repeat what he said.

WINTER
Racing in the margins

The white face of the Euro peloton has gone, and with it the idea of seasons. Long-haul flights confuse any idea of time of year. 40 degree heat in Malaysia, zero in China, the Fall in southern Africa. Welcome to the UCI Continentals.

The racing is similar to home, but so different, truly global: Australians, Japanese, Malaysians, Iranians, Irishmen... even Azerbaijanis. It's an international interzone of pro bike racing.

Some riders are on the way up, moving towards a pro tour contract. Some on the way down – riders that were in a top-flight team the previous year, tasted the good stuff, didn't make the cut and lost their contracts. They are angry.

Some racers are on the comeback trail. Brought down with injury maybe, they are fighting their way back up, showing what they have. But they're in the last chance saloon. Others are good racers that could have been domestiques on the world tour, but in the interzone they have a chance of podium action. All this, and a sprinkling of racers on their limit – perhaps they're policemen in their 9-5 – getting the chance to ride a big race.

There was a chance there were some supercharged riders from donkey farms in one of the 'stan nations.

It's bandit country, right down to the 'team cars' – budget hire-car Hyundais in sponsor stickers. I've seen a DS in the back seat asleep and the mechanic driving. I've seen elephants crossing... and my life flash before my eyes in these team hire cars.

It's a culture clash. Iranians sneaking beer into their rooms; Brits struggling with breakfast in 40 degrees. The Euro scene is as far away as Iran from Japan; Australia from Africa. Welcome to the margins.

Shut eye on the red eye
Irishman Matt Brammeier en route to South Africa for the Mzansi Tour. You can tell it's Air Ethiopia because none of the interior seats match.

Bogs and embrocation
It doesn't matter whether it's a village hall in Essex, or 40 degrees in Malaysia – bike racers still perform the same pre-race ritual.

Behind closed doors

I'd never seen bicycles outside hotel doors before – until now. I don't know whether the riders left them there, or the team mechanics.

Signing in
The Tour de Langkawi, 2014

Above
Roadside ritual
Baku riders doing weird strangeness in the
pounding heat before the start.

Opposite top
Race pins
The universal act of attaching race numbers
with good old-fashioned safety pins is seen
the world over – at all levels of competition.

Opposite below
Just awkward
The three jersey wearers sit uncomfortably
on the start line as Malaysian dancers
perform a traditional pre-race knees up.

Overleaf
Mzansi Tour, South Africa, 2014
A rare, for me, ground-level shot as the
peloton rolls out at the start of stage 2.

Previous pages

Elevated company

p218-219: I was looking for somewhere high
to shoot from – and found a huge
ornamental bridge with a walkway over
the top. My vantage point revealed
how the Malaysian rain forest had been
butchered on an industrial scale.

Peloton – Langkawi style

p220-221: A familiar line of riders,
familiar roadside fans – but all a bit strange.
All a bit Malaysian.

This page

Protecting the leader's jersey

The Iranians are drilling it in the oil field.

Overleaf

End of the earth

This is definitely not your normal finish line.
It's got all the usual UCI race furniture –
the banners, the inflatable arch – but here,
there's no grandstand, dignitaries or even
team buses. But the Golden Gate Highlands
National Park, South Africa, is stunning,
really quite beautiful.

Above

Mzansi Tour, South Africa, 2014

Winning is winning... but this is a brutally
empty finish..

Opposite

Out in front

Winning in The Golden Gate Highlands
National Park, South Africa, Janse Van
Rensburg didn't even have the peloton for
company at the finish.

Overleaf

Exhausted. Hot. Snapped

Cannonball sprinter, Michael Schweiser,
somewhere in Malaysia. He'd hit the
deck earlier in the race and the Asia-based
press corps want their pound of flesh.

Opposite top

Selamat Datang

Baku rider, Elchin Asadov is unaware
that he has chosen to compose himself at
the stage finish outside a local brothel.

Opposite below

Road rash

Michael Schweiser has come down.

Overleaf

If you can't stand the heat...

It's so hot in Langkawi that fire crews attend
the finish lines to hose the riders cool.
I saw the shot, just dived in with my camera.
And got soaked for my trouble.

OUTRO
Camille McMillan: Correspondent

Looking at the Tour de France, it's glamorous: colour, suntans and sunglasses, bikes sparkling, TV crews jostling – bustling in to a town for a night, off again at dawn.

Except that it's not.

Like the clichéd clown, under the facade it's lonely, isolating. There are battles in the race, battles in the hotel, battles on the team buses. Egos rage. Riders are tired, always tired, with the attrition of racing, eating, sleeping. There are long hours, grabbed sleep, fears over form, illness or injury.

And the never-ending road heaps on the fatigue. Always the road, sucking the marrow, sapping the energy away. But it's addictive. The racers are gladiators, they are performers: professionals in a circus.

It's not just the riders who tire, the entire team shares the fatigue of the road: the drivers, soigneurs, mechanics, cooks and the TV and radio crews. And also me – the photographer. The riders don't know this, they think they are the only tired ones. Don't ever tell them, they'll get upset. Misguidedly, they think they are the reason for the race. They are not.

I like to remind them sometimes that 80% of the people at the roadside of Le Tour come for the publicity caravan, to be showered with the souvenirs chucked out from the crazy caravan of vehicles following the race. They're not there for the 30 seconds of riders spitting, swearing, glittering, thundering or promenading past.

There are other races with glamour. The Giro d'Italia, the Monuments, the Classics. There are minor tours and hundreds of day races that are not famous outside of cycling connoisseurs. They are full of the stories that all races have, but less... soul sucking. All these small races feed the bigger races. They are where the riders train, where team managers spot riders for the next event – dress rehearsals for the Tour de France: the Big Top.

But as a whole, bike racing on mainland Europe is dying, dying like the working class people who watched it. Minor races in Belgium or the Basque country have small crowds, gaggles of old men hanging around the start watching Lycra-clad riders (it can be quite unnerving). Sometimes these small 'Fish and Chip' races have no spectators at all, save the occasional oddball in the middle of nowhere, with no apparent means of reaching that destination.

There are a few photographers that follow all the races and are part of the circus all season long. There are the pillion-riding photomotos in shirtsleeves, helmeted with cameras hanging from their shoulders like speed-addicted gauchos. These reporters will be with the race all day, picking photogenic vistas or guessing where race 'moments' will be. After the race they head to the press room, hunching over computers to upload their images to the wire. They are the motorcycle gang: without the studded leathers but just as impossible to join.

There are other photographers that work for big photo agencies that seem to appear only for Le Tour. They only focus on the team stars.

And there are the weird big guys, full of press lunches at the arrival village. They work the finish line with huge zoom lenses, focusing solely on the moment the winner touches the line. As jaded as porn cameramen, the moment the winner hits the line is the only money shot for them.

This too is the age of the 'embedded ' photographer, hired to record every waking moment of a team's riders. Just like photographers embedded with troops in wartime, there is a cost to that great access: ▷

Opposite

Critérium du Dauphiné

The ascent of one of the classic Alpine passes in the Critérium du Dauphiné, 2008 – the riders working their way up to the famous Croix de Fer, and the fans who watch them. And the motos who stalk them...

235

One rider thought he could do it on 20 minutes sleep a night. Then his neck gave out after 23 hours holding his head up. So did he give up? No, he gaffer-taped his entire head to his neck to keep it in place. Stories don't come much better than that...

◁ a news filter passes over the shots, there is an agenda. Embedded photographers appeared as a reaction to the hardly earth-shattering news of Lance Armstrong. Teams wanted to show 'behind the scenes', to reveal how the riders lived, and how clean they were. I'm sure we can all trust a photographer paid by the team to give us complete transparency on that one.

These guys quickly get sucked into the world of secrecy and sponsorship requests, stylising the riders, making the artistes look hyper-heroic and epic. Embedded photographers move away from photo-journalism very quickly (if there ever were such photographers).

I have seen photographers altering a scene to give the required result. Photoshop mostly, pornification with HDR and selective sharpening. Sometimes it's taken further. I witnessed two old hands chatting in the shower block (a holy space to cycling) at the finish of the Paris-Roubaix. The rider was small-talking with a cameraman, then it happened. The photographer readied, the rider got back in the shower cubical and proceeded to pose with an *'I look f*cked'* face, head in hand. The 'epic shot' was in the bag.

I'm not saying all pictures are staged of course: the sport is brutal and sometimes deadly, but there is a masquerade.

However, in the same way some racers have doped for enhanced performance, so too are some of the photographs – photodoping?

I once told an embedded photographer the story of the staged shower shot. He told me, with some pride, how he had 'art directed' a particular shot – of a discarded *maillot jaune* – by picking it up and moving it to create a more perfect composition.

He thought that was cool. How do I know? Well I've been embedded myself. I never altered a scene.

Which is probably why, after the first year, I never did it again. Ever.

Jaded? Maybe. For a time, bike racing lost its shine for me. The gloss of the Tour de France, the hyperbole of the Spring Classics, super-teams with PR banality and brand guideline overkill. I was just getting bored of it all.

But then something happened to reignite my love of cycling photography: the Transcontinental Race: 2,600 miles from Belgium to Istanbul.

It's a huge feat: a long race that is somehow slow cycling – no support vehicles, no teams, you choose your route – and some unbelievable individual stories. The winner managed it in less than ten days with about two hours' sleep in a field en route. There was a month between the winner and the guy who came last.

One rider thought he could do it on 20 minutes sleep a night. Then his neck gave out after 23 hours holding his head up. So did he give up? No, he gaffer-taped his entire head to his neck to keep it in place. Stories don't come much better than that. And there are so many.

With so many kilometers, such hunger, different routes, sleep deprivation, mechanicals and savage stray dogs along the way, it's inevitable every rider tells a story.

I wonder if it is the future of cycling? It's more contemporary than the Grand Tours with its great online presence. And more 'mindful', if you like. Trendy expression I know, but it fits: being where you are, rather than riding a wave of adrenaline. The TCR plumbs the origins of cycling. The Grand Tours are getting colder and colder with their lead-out trains and marginal gains. But the Trans was both fresh, and had legacy. It taps into the past, and points to the future.

It suits me. I'm not the pro photographer at the pro races looking to glam up the show or looking for the epic mountain shot with a rider screwing up his face like a cat's ar*e. I look for the epic in the everyday, in the banality of it.

But that's fine. That's how it is.

I am a Correspondent.　◆

Trancontinental legends

James Hayden, *top*, led from the start and pushed himself hard. Trying to finish and with a final roll of the dice he attempted to alleviate his neck issues with tape. *Chapeau!*

Walter Reiterer, *above*, rode the 2,600 mile Transcontinental race in printed lederhosen. He was, to my trained eye, mad as a brush. I liked him. Everyone was plagued by stray dogs on the race, chasing, nipping and putting the fear of God into them. Walter had the solution: he carried a rock. The next attack, he used it, and dispatched the snarling hound back to hell.

And that's what that race did for me, it dispatched my dogs back to hell.

I would like to thank the following people, without whom the creation of this book would not have been possible:

Paul and Katy
Milly and Rhett

And the generous Kickstarter donors:

Mark McCabe
Martin Cox

Paul Acomb
Stephen Baillie
Dean Brett
Alastair Dickie
Erik Johansen
John Fisher
Kevin Franklin
James Lumpkin
Dave Murray
Marie Paulsson
Mat Pennell
Hugh Watters

James Atkins
James Beardon
Jeff Biss
Kathryn Brown
Gabbi Cahane
Tim Cheshire
Victoria Conran
Andrew Croker
Mark Culmer
Robert Davies
Dean Downing
Rohan Dubash
Bernhard Eisel
James Fairbank
Sarah Farmer
Gary Fryett
Debbie Ghant

Jordan Gibbons,
William Gilchrist
Justin Greenleaf
Andrew Heaney
Neil Hendry
Kristian House
David Iberson-Hurst
Moyeen Islam
MJ Jackson
Matt Johnson
Rob Jonas
Phil Judge
Gavin Law
Max Leonard
Steve Makin
Neil Manning
Stuart Mayell
Avril Millar
David Millar
Ilona Niinivirta
Kevin Oakhill
Charlie Pearch
Gareth Quinn
Brendan Quirk
Kristof Ramon
Martin Rhodes
Mick Riley
Richard Rounding
Greg Rowe
Wilson Sim
Chris Tree
Allister Tulett

Robert Allan
Andreas Braukmann
David Craig
James Edwards
Henry Engels
Paul Fairbairn
Toby Gallagher
Andrew Marks
and Shaun Roche

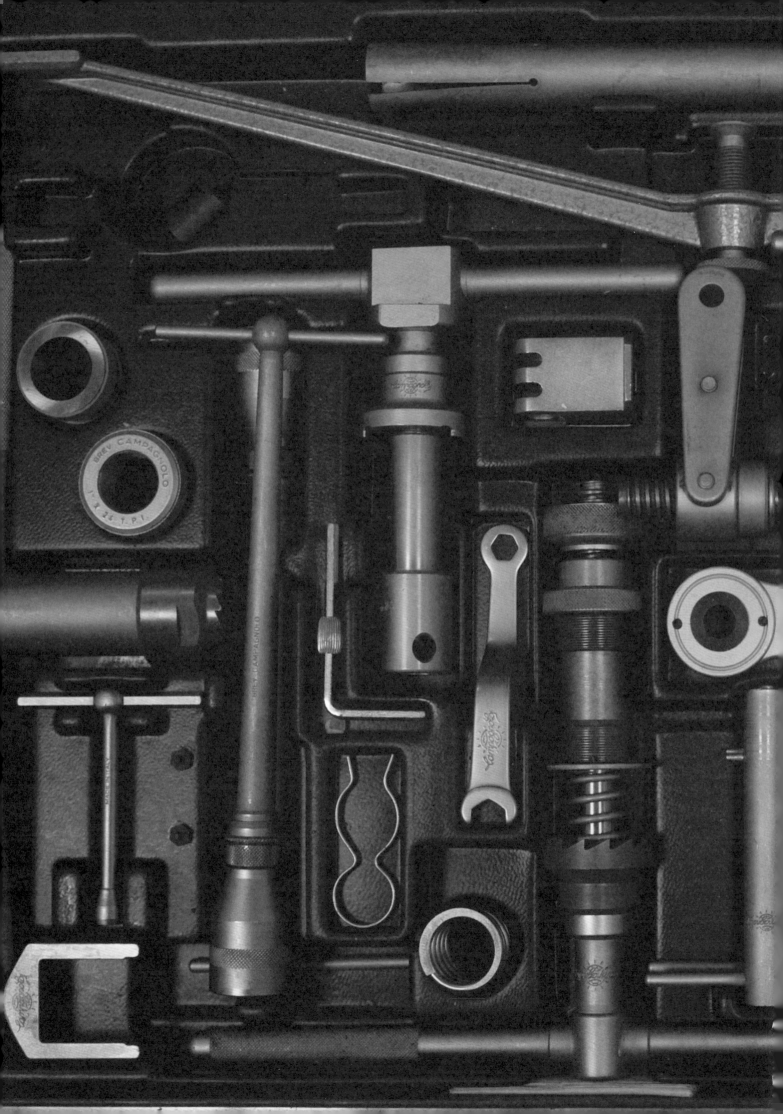